Rediscovering..

The

ORPINGTON

Car

THE DEFINITIVE GUIDE

Trevor Mulligan

Rediscovering...

The

ORPINGTON

Car

THE DEFINITIVE GUIDE

Trevor Mulligan

INDEX

COPYRIGHT NOTICE

DEDICATION

To my dear wife, Myra, who thought I was bonkers when I told her that I wanted to research the Orpington car and then write a book about it. Still, she did let me get on with it, for which I am grateful.

Specially designed for low cost of upkeep

10 h.p. Two-seater with large Dickey

THE BUSINESS MAN'S CAR

ECONOMICAL :: RELIABLE :: SPEEDY

Sole Concessionaires:

G.N.U. Motor & Accessories Co, Westbourne Grove, London, W2.

Manufacturers:

Smith & Milroy, Ltd, Orpington, Kent.

The Business Man's Car promotional sales advertisement
Picture courtesy of Pamela Moate.

ACKNOWLEDGEMENTS

Without the contributions of the following, this publication might not have been put together. My thanks therefore go to the people and organisations listed.

Mrs Pamela Moate of Woodchurch, Kent, the granddaughter of Frank Smith, for her invaluable input and loan supply of previously-unpublished information and photographs.

Philip Babbs, who is not only one of my fellow supporters of Cray Wanderers FC, the oldest association football club in London which was founded in nearby St Mary Cray in 1860, but is also a direct relative of Frank Smith who was the designer of the Orpington.

Edward Babbs, Phil's father and the nephew of Frank Smith, for correcting some background information in his excellent article on the Orpington car, and allowing me to refer to its contents.

Jerry Dowlen, author of several books, and historian at Cray Wanderers FC, who encouraged me to sit down at my computer and start formulating this book.

Phil Waller, whose Orpington History website at **www.orpington-history.org** I accidentally found one day. Phil helped greatly by grabbing some important photos for me when I was unable to visit Bromley Library.

Bromley Library, for retaining historical articles and photos relating to the Orpington car.

Marie-Louise Kerr (Curator) of the Bromley Museum in Orpington. My thanks for providing the image of the enamel car badge which has been reproduced in monochrome on page 100 and in colour on the outer back cover of this book.

Mick Harris, George Smith, Laurie Crawford and **Peter Dench**, who all replied to my letter printed in the CSMA's *Motoring & Leisure* magazine in 2008 (in which I requested further information on the Orpington car), even though the information they all supplied was already known by me; their response was much appreciated.

INTRODUCTION

I very first heard about the Orpington car when I was in my early teens in the late 1960s yet, like so many other local readers, I read an article in the *Orpington & Kentish Times* and then recycled the newspaper. But, it's one of those niggling matters that never went away, so in 2008 I decided to find out more about the car. How surprised I was at the apparent lack of information that was readily available on this subject – and how contradictory that limited information was. So much so that I decided to research it myself and, with the aid of Frank Smith's family, this book is the outcome.

During my research into the Orpington car, I have had the privilege of speaking with and meeting Mrs Pamela Moate, the granddaughter of Mr Frank Smith, the designer of this vehicle, and I was given access to a number of facts and photographs that appear to have been overlooked by the writers of previous articles on the car. Because of this, I have managed to add further information on the people directly involved with the Orpington car and the company that was behind it, Smith & Milroy Ltd.

Then, just when I thought I'd gathered everything possible to include within these pages, a chance introduction to Phil Waller (the researcher behind the Orpington History website) led to some more photographs being accessed.

This book started life as a very short but factual few pages but, as I met the family of Frank Smith and they presented me with historical items, the 12 or so pages booklet that I had planned to publish suddenly began to grow in volume.

Although there's been quite a few articles written about the Orpington car in the past, there's never been a keepsake publication that motor car enthusiasts can place on their bookshelves alongside the more well-known and enduring marques of yesteryear that are still around today. Of the previous articles that have been written about the Orpington car, most – no, *all* - of them (with the exception of, perhaps, the specialist motoring magazines of the 1920s) have been inaccurate in a material particular regarding one 'fact' or another. This could be down to something simple like the writer not quite researching their facts properly, or maybe they couldn't find a particular piece of the puzzle so they've guessed and got it wrong. This book, which covers the most comprehensive information ever assembled in one place on the Orpington car and its originators, aims to set the record straight once and for all.

I don't profess to being an expert on cars or anything mechanical but, with the information provided to me and through my own research, I have been able to piece together the correct information necessary to write this publication.

The Orpington car was a trendsetter, trailblazer and an innovation in its time. I'll now leave you to read all about it.

Trevor Mulligan

HOW IT ALL BEGAN

Let me please try and set the scene for you. At the turn of the 19th into the 20th century, Queen Victoria still ruled the land. Her life, though, was coming to an end and the country was awaiting the succession of Edward VII to the throne. Motoring, a luxury hobby in those days, was just starting to catch on and there were only about 8,000 car owners throughout Britain.

Motor vehicle usage on the sparse road network began to increase during the next 20 years, jumping in popularity during the 1920s with the introduction and manufacture of smaller, cheaper, lightweight vehicles.

One little-known and overlooked car was also born in 1920 but, nowadays, many people have probably never heard of it. Yet, in yesteryear, it was a potential market leader in its field. That was the Orpington car.

Back in 1907, two cousins in the north-west Kent town had an idea about creating a home-

Rediscovering... The ORPINGTON Car

1920 Motor Show Promotional Card

Enjoying a day out in an Orpington

Pictures courtesy of Pamela Moate.

18

produced motor car in England that was reliable and comfortable.

Frank Smith and John Milroy actually started their firm up four years earlier in 1903. In similar fashion to the more well-known partnership of Messrs Rolls and Royce, Messrs Smith and Milroy also started out initially as bicycle builders and repairers in the nearby village of Crockenhill, where Frank Smith's father owned a grocer's shop. John 'Jack' Milroy was actually Frank's cousin, although he wasn't a local lad. He'd travelled south from his native Stranraer in Scotland and both men were also the best of friends as well as blood relatives.

However, it was in 1907 that they produced the first of their own vehicles. By then they were working from premises in Wellington Road, St Mary Cray, a property that was owned by Frank's mother. The vehicle that they created was a 5cwt, solid tyre, light delivery van (shown on page 20). Whether or not the vehicle was actually commissioned, or whether it was provided by the cousins for promotional purposes, is no longer clear but the recipient of the van was the Orpington Hand Laundry of Chislehurst Road in the town.

In 1912, Frank and Jack transferred their business from its humble beginnings in Wellington Road, to larger premises opposite

The 1907 Smith & Milroy 5cwt Light Van parked outside the Wellington Road workshop.
Photo sourced by Phil Waller, Orpington History website.

the Priory Gardens pond (the source of the River Cray), a little way along from the Carlton Parade shops, on the corner of Perry Hall Road and Orpington High Street. As I write this, the site is now a 'Texaco' petrol station; when I was growing up in the area, it was a 'Regent' petrol station and, after I had learned to drive in the early 1970s, I took my first two or three cars there for MOT tests.

Primitive though it may sound to us all now, the High Street premises in 1912 were powered with light by a gas engine and dynamo. This 'state of the art technology' (if the phrase was even thought of back then) made them the first

business in Orpington to use this type of lighting.

Everything was bubbling along nicely until the interruption caused by the First World War.

Partly because things happened so quickly, half of the Smith and Milroy workforce got sucked into battle, willingly or otherwise. The call-ups included one for Jack Milroy. Fortunately, all of

A Smith & Milroy name plate
Picture courtesy of Edward Babbs.

Smith & Milroy workshop in Orpington High St, 1915
Photo courtesy of Phil Waller, Orpington History website

the employees of the company who went to war returned without injury, although several contracted an illness – probably the Spanish 'flu, which was rife during that mighty conflict and which has been reported on numerous occasions as having killed more people than the war did itself.

THE WAR YEARS 1914-1918

The employees that stayed behind, when the others went off to fight for King and Country, found that they had to adapt to making weapon parts for the war effort.

Smith and Milroy had adapted their works into making parts for trench bombs, rifle grenades and fuses. It was reported that as many as 6,000 items were produced each week by the workers, who were covering a 24-hours shift roster.

Interestingly, during the 'Great War', Frank Smith's youngest of seven sisters drove the parts from Orpington to London. Being one of the first women drivers, from 1914 Miss Katie Smith (later to become Mrs Babbs and then Mrs Scott-Murray) made regular trips to the City to ensure prompt delivery of the items to the War Office.

It is unclear what vehicle she used, but perhaps it could have been that the company borrowed back the 1907 van that they had built and presented to the Orpington Hand Laundry or, equally, it could have been the much larger panelled van in which Frank Smith in later years took his family on holidays and day trips.

Without documented proof or even a photograph, this must be considered conjecture on my part, but neither possibility should be ruled out. It's just a pity that the partnership or company records no longer appear to exist from way back then, otherwise we would all know for certain.

WHAT HAPPENED NEXT

The end of the war brought an increased demand for personal motor vehicle transportation. In 1918, the company increased its covered floor space with extra buildings, in order to cope with the additional work that was necessary.

Progression was very swift and, upon the arrival of 1920, the new decade brought with it the revelation that the Smith and Milroy company was finalising the design and production of its own vehicle called, quite simply, the Orpington.

Finished in French-grey, the car sported a single bench seat for two occupants and a 'dickey' seat in the boot which could accommodate another two people as and when the need arose.

As was generally the case back in days of yore, this vehicle used a dynamo to power its lights.

Rediscovering... The ORPINGTON Car

The previous reports I have read about this car strongly indicate that it was a pleasure to drive, extremely comfortable and easy on the steering. Considering the apparent lack of luxury suspension back then, I would say that the comfort aspect related to something like a vast improvement on riding on a horse and cart!

Choice of colours for the Orpington car: French-grey only
Photo courtesy of Pamela Moate.

It's estimated (more like guestimated) that only around 20 to 25 of these little cars were built and sold between 1920 and 1924 (or 1925, depending on which account you read), due eventually to the introduction of mass-producing car manufacturers like Ford flooding the market and driving Smith and Milroy's Orpington out of the picture.

Whilst it is understood that Smith and Milroy aimed to keep production and sales costs of the Orpington affordably low, in the end they just couldn't compete with the big boys who were able to undercut them on price and beat them hands down on productivity.

Smith and Milroy continued after the demise of the Orpington but reportedly no longer competed in the vehicle manufacture race. In fact, in 1927, their business proved once more not to have a Luddite approach when they installed an innovative shilling slot machine on their forecourt for the sale of their petrol to the general public.

Rediscovering... The ORPINGTON Car

Staff members line up outside the Smith & Milroy Ltd workshop. Also in view are a Model T Ford (left of picture) and a tinplate cutout of a saluting AA Patrolman (far right of the picture).

Another group shot of the staff and management of Smith & Milroy. I have circled and labelled Frank Smith and Jack Milroy

Photos courtesy of Pamela Moate

THE TECHNICAL BIT

No book on a motor car can be complete without stating the technical attributes that go towards making it drive on the roads.

I must admit here that I occasionally find this part of a motoring book quite boring, especially if a motoring 'anorak' has written the dialogue. However, I aim to spare you the misfortune of falling asleep mid-sentence, as I can claim to be a bit of a football 'anorak' but this generally doesn't spill over onto other subjects.

I will further admit that, without me first having researched the subject of the Orpington and gleaned the following information, you probably wouldn't be reading a chapter entitled 'The Technical Bit'!

So, let's all breathe in, and I'll begin…

The Orpington, in common with several other makes of car at the time, shared certain Model T Ford parts such as brakes, steering and axles.

This, together with the following components, resulted in the Orpington being one of the most economical and spacious vehicles on the market.

The Orpington's Specifications:

Four cylinders, 10-12hp

66mm Bore

Stroke 110mm (1498cc)

Weight complete: 12cwt (two-seater)

12.5cwt (four-seater)

Side by side valves

Transmission by shaft

Three speeds

Right hand drive steering

Fabric Cone Clutch

Approximate consumption: 40mpg

Rediscovering... **The ORPINGTON Car**

Six-gallon capacity fuel tank

Thermo-siphon cooling system

Force-fed pump and splash lubrication

Separate gearbox construction

Straight bevel back axle drive

Semi-elliptic front and rear springing

710 x 90mm tyres on steel wheels

Zenith carburettor

Magneto ignition

Maximum speed: 'speedy'

Looking at those specifics, it would seem that the Orpington was quite a nippy little roadster for its time. Indeed, I have little doubt that it may even have given some modern-day medium range hatchbacks a good run for their money.

The engine used in the Orpington was manufactured by the Coventry Simplex company, which was well known at the time of the Kent car's construction. The Orpington, as specifically designed by Frank Smith, was to allow for the car's owners to purchase spare parts with the least amount of waiting time and without having to approach the parent firm. The Coventry Simplex parts were readily available in the 1920s, whereas the gearbox and steering assembly were a standard make at that time.

The more I researched this little car, the more I began to realise what a shrewd, but extremely clever, person Frank Smith was. He had literally designed a car with popular parts from other manufacturers in mind and then all his and Jack Milroy's work force had to do was to build the vehicles knowing that the prospective buyers wouldn't have to worry about any possible shortage of spares.

The original price of the Orpington was £225 for the two-seater and the four-seater waded in at another £25. Purchase tax on both vehicles was listed at £11. A later reference I found, gave the cost as £395 for the chassis and £495 for the standard two-seater. Both were sold as separate items; that is to say, the chassis only was £395 but, for an extra £100, the two-seater bodywork was added.

By pricing the chassis only and chassis with bodywork separately, Smith and Milroy were able to supply other motor traders and coachbuilders with the chassis only in order to allow for different car bodies to be added. Also, the difference between the two-seater and the four-seater versions was the 'dickey' seat in the boot. An either/or optional extra.

Maybe because of the low-volume turnover of completely built cars emanating from the Smith and Milroy factory, they only had one sales dealership which was described in motoring publications from the 1920s as a 'concessionaire'. This was the G.N.U. Motor and Accessories Company of Westbourne Grove, London W2 – quite a stone's throw away from the town of Orpington itself. Unfortunately for them, G.N.U. lost the agency in 1922 due to the lack of sales that they generated.

I have included more technical data on the next few pages, courtesy of magazine articles handed to me whilst I was compiling the contents of this book.

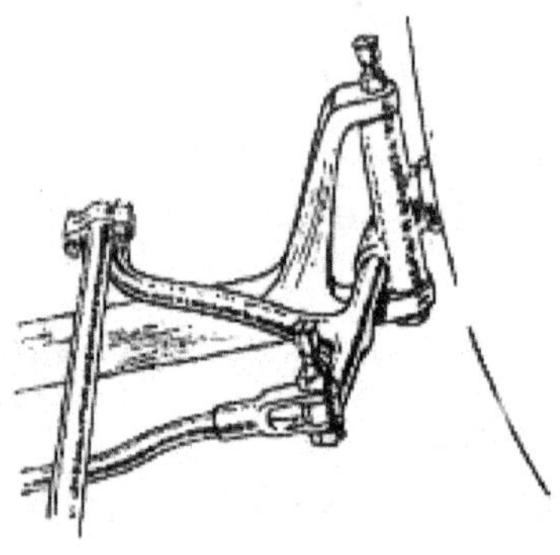

Steering details of the Orpington car (above) with a view of the engine and transmission (below). Pictures courtesy of Frank Smith's family archives.

WHAT *THE AUTOCAR* MAGAZINE SAID

I've reproduced below an excerpt from *The Autocar* magazine, dated November 27th 1920. It was the first year of production of the Orpington and, as is often the case nowadays, reviews of the cars of the time were featured in the motoring publications that existed. Unfortunately, I don't know who the author of the review was, but in three paragraphs (the only part of what was a fuller review that I wasn't able to access in its entirety) the writer appears to have summed up the Orpington quite succinctly.

> "So far as ordinary main roads are concerned, the Orpington slipped along at a good average without effort and practically noiselessly, and gear changing in traffic was not awkward, although double clutching is necessary in changing down, as on a good many other cars. The foot brake, operating on a drum behind

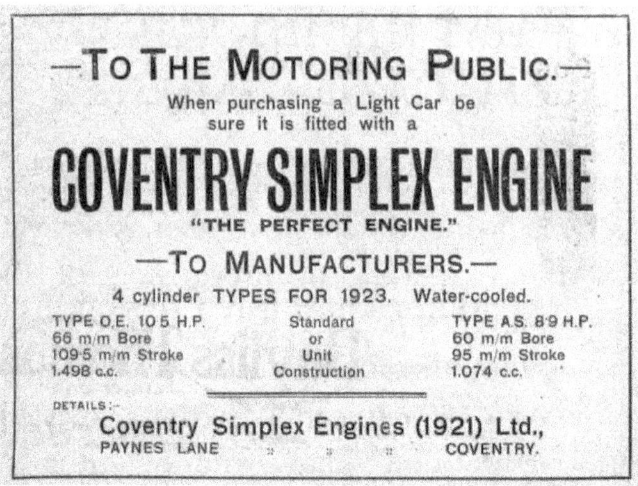

Two Coventry Simplex engine advertisements from the 1920s.
Pictures courtesy of Frank Smith's family archives.

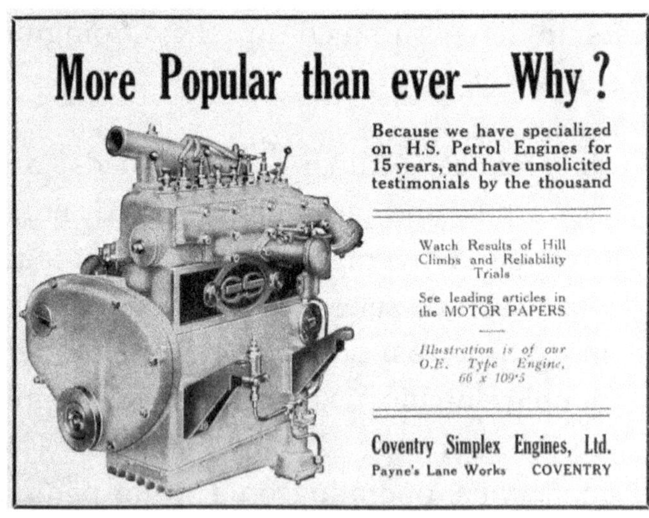

the gear box, was powerful but somewhat harsh, whereas the side brake controlling the expanding shoes in the rear wheel drums was sweet in action, but insufficiently decisive for emergency purposes, both matters for adjustment only. An excellent point in this car is the lightness of the steering, the fingers only being required to effect all the necessary movement of the steering wheel, and the control is in no way affected or jolted by very bad road surfaces, such as we found in the South of London, and in cart tracks and lanes in Surrey.

"A folding dickey seat at the rear allows of two extra passengers being carried, and as the back of this seat is high the additional passengers are well protected from dust or dirt at the rear. Incidentally, the passengers do not occupy an elevated position, thereby allowing of protection against draught by the hood.

"A Tredelect electric lighting set is fitted as standard with two medium sized headlights on the front wings, indicating the full width of the car to oncomers at night time. Both dynamo and accumulator are accessible, the former being located alongside the gear box and the latter in the locker at the rear."

The Orpington Car on Esher Common, Surrey,
between London and Brooklands, circa 1920.
Picture courtesy of Frank Smith's family archives.

A pretty much descriptive account of how enjoyable an experience it appears to have been to drive the Orpington car.

Rediscovering... The ORPINGTON Car

On the following pages I have reproduced original articles from *The Motor* magazine and *Light Car and Cyclecar* magazine. I have retyped the content of both articles, because the photocopied pages I received are just barely readable as they are, but wouldn't be legible if I just copied and pasted the photocopies onto the pages of this publication.

THE COMPLETE ARTICLE
AS PUBLISHED IN
THE MOTOR MAGAZINE
ON 3 NOVEMBER 1920

The Orpington Light Car

A New Model Expressly Designed for the Owner-Driver

Amongst the newcomers this year into the lighter class of cars is the 10hp Orpington light car, the sole concessionaries for which are the G.N.U. Motor and Accessories Co., Westbourne House, Westbourne Grove, London W2. Perhaps the outstanding features of this machine lie in its sturdy construction and exceptionally well-finished bodywork.

Scientific Price Reduction

The main effort of the manufacturers has been to produce a machine at a reasonable figure, whilst at the same time it incorporates a high degree of comfort. With a view to reducing the difficulty of obtaining spare parts, whether in this country or overseas, many standard Ford components have been used in its construction.

The power unit, which needs no introduction, is a Coventry-Simplex, the bore and stroke of the cylinders being 66mm by 109.5mm, dimensions which give a cubic capacity of 1500cc. Cooling is on the thermo-syphonic principle, the radiator employed being of the honeycomb type and giving the machine a substantial and prepossessing appearance. The mixture is supplied by a Zenith carburettor, controlled by an accelerator fitted with a convenient form of roller-type pedal. Interconnected with this pedal is a wire terminating in a ring which is carried forward to a point just below the radiator, so that during the process of starting up the engine the throttle can be conveniently operated. Ignition is provided for by a M.L magneto, the advance and retard lever of which is secured to the steering column just below the wheel.

The clutch, which is particularly smooth in action, is of the Ferodo-lined cone type. The drive from this is taken by a fabric type universal joint to a Moss three-speed-and-reverse gearbox, the control lever for which is fitted in the orthodox position on the right-hand side of the driver, working on the usual form of gate.

From the gearbox the drive to the bevel-driven rear axle is by an enclosed propeller shaft, one large-diameter fabric-type universal joint being provided at its forward end. The suspension is carried out by flat semi-elliptics in front and splayed quarter-elliptics at the rear. The wheels, which are of the Sankey detachable type, are shod with 710mm by 90mm tyres. Braking is provided for by two independently-operated sets of brakes, that connected to the pedal being of the contracting type operating on a drum situated immediately behind the gearbox, whilst the lever brakes are of an internal-expanding type operating within drums secured to the rear wheels.

Starter Motor Unnecessary

Steering is carried out by means of worm and full worm wheel mechanism, a very desirable feature being found in the sturdy stay extending from the dash to the steering column, which serves to give rigidity to the latter, thus eliminating any suggestion of dither at the wheel. Dynamo lighting forms a standard fitting on the Orpington, for which the Tredelect instrument is responsible. The body, which is finished in French grey, has fairly high sides and back, and therefore provides that needful support to the shoulders which is so often lacking. The upholstery is very generous, a feature which adds considerably to the comfort of the passengers. A dickey seat, capable of accommodating two persons, is formed in the boot of the machine, whilst ample room for spare parts and tools is provided beneath the seat. The price of the Orpington complete with spare wheel, hood, screen, tools, etc., is £495.

THE TEST RUN ARTICLE AS PUBLISHED IN *THE LIGHT CAR AND CYCLECAR* MAGAZINE ON 6 NOVEMBER 1920

In the above-mentioned issue of *The Light Car and Cyclecar* magazine, the description of the Orpington's attributes was very similarly worded to *The Motor* magazine article dated three days earlier (see previous chapter), giving rise to the possibility that both magazines were either issued by the same publisher or, that they copied the information from a press release prepared by Smith & Milroy Ltd for publicity purposes.

However, where this article deviated from *The Motor* magazine version was the inclusion of a road test report on the Orpington. I have therefore skipped the first part already similarly covered and have reproduced the write-up of the test run result in its entirety.

"Having seen to its petrol, oil and water supplies, we headed the Orpington towards the first test hill. We were soon held up, however, as our photographer was having a "day out" with his machine, and it cost us an hour before we could proceed. Ranmore Common is a fair climb, the difficulty in surmounting it being found in an acute left-hand turn, the gradient thereabouts being a 1 in 6. The Orpington left a third of the hill behind it before a change of gear became necessary, and second gear saw us making excellent headway towards the bend. Some few yards from the turn the gradient steepens suddenly, and coming down to first we were able to take the bend at our ease. The bend negotiated, we speeded up the engine and changed up into second gear, in which gear the climb was finished. We have little doubt that with the engine well run in Ranmore Common would represent a second gear climb in the Orpington.

"A pleaseant run over the "switchback", a second gear climb to the top of White Downs, and the radiator literally disappeared from view as the dangerous descent of White Downs was commenced. "Safety First" being our motto, we slipped the gear lever into first, and by disengaging the clutch we were able to test the respective merits of the independently controlled brakes. The hand brake was certainly positive in action, but the foot brake, which, as has been mentioned, is of the transmission type, was scarcely up to its work, and, as we soon discovered, was in need of adjustment only.

"The villages of Abinger, Gomshall and Shere could never have looked more picturesque than they did on this October day. Everywhere the golden tints of Autumn lent a richness to the countryside, whilst here and there splashes of green stood out, defying the hand of Nature. We were compelled to speed on, however, as we had not too much light before us, and we were soon at the foot of Coombe Bottom. The manner in which the Orpington pulled on top gear on this gradient was a welcome surprise to us, and we were enabled to reach the second acute bend before we found it necessary to change gear. In second the machine made comparatively light work of the climb until the "hair-pin", with its 1 in 5 gradient, hove in sight, when we were compelled to come down into first. The surface on the bend was exceptionally loose and did not help the machine in its climb, but the Orpington did not show the slightest hesitation, and we were able to take the bend with ease and certainty.

"From Coombe Bottom to Pebble Coombe, by a circuitous route via Newlands Corner, there was nothing to worry the machine, but we had an opportunity of being able to appreciate its really excellent suspension. The

Orpington is one of the few machines that is not worried by pot holes or boulders, and we did not feel the slightest discomfort when traversing that very indifferent by-way which we have named the "Marshes". Although the springing serves effectively to absorb road shock, there is a certain amount of body sway present which proves somewhat disconcerting, and which in our opinion, could be easily overcome.

"Passing through Dorking and Betchworth, we were soon at the foot of Pebble Coombe, the last test hill on the course. This hill is practically straight and of good surface, but represents a first gear climb for most machines, as it has a maximum gradient of about 1 in 5. After making good headway, first on top and then on second, the Orpington reached the summit in its first gear with plenty of power in hand. The top of Pebble Coombe practically represents the end of the test, as the drop down Box Hill to Burford Bridge presents no difficulty.

"The outstanding feature of the Orpington undoubtedly lies in the amount of comfort which it provides, for which the springing and high backed seats are responsible. The bevel was rather inclined to be noisy, but the clutch and gearbox leave nothing to be desired."

Rediscovering... The ORPINGTON Car

*The Orpington bypassing a larger car during the
'Light Car and Cyclecar' test run in 1920.*

*Taking the turn towards White Downs, after a successful
ascent of Ranmore Common*

Photos courtesy of Frank Smith's family archives.

NEWSPAPER ARTICLES

The Orpington Times and its predecessor, *The Orpington & Kentish Times*, appear to hold prominence in this area with no less than three separate articles (there may be more, although undiscovered as I write this) published on the Orpington car.

The first report on the Orpington appeared in the *Kentish Times* dated 9 January 1959 (*image, left*). One major surprise to stand out was that the reporter added a footnote that said he had 'spent some time on research for it' and then stated that he couldn't

trace a photograph of an Orpington!

He couldn't have looked very far, because several motoring magazines from the 1920s onwards featured photographs of the car, and Bromley Library held *(and still hold)* back issues of the *Kentish Times* group of local newspapers, in which the reporter would have undoubtedly found a picture of the car had he researched the subject as stated.

Another article that I saw was the one from the *Orpington Times* dated 14 August 1980. This was to prove to be the most controversial article to date, claiming that an Orpington was adapted for the 'handicapped son of a rich Arab'. The photocopy of the report that I was shown had the paragraph stating this snippet of information marked in

ink. Attached to the photocopied page was a note typed on pastel green paper by one of Frank Smith's (by then grown up) children, which introduced the possibility – even probability - that it may not have been an Orpington after all that had been adapted, but instead a Rolls Royce. You can read all about this matter, under the chapter headed *'The Adapted Car – And What Really Happened'* on page 79.

HAND MADE: The Orpington Car, produced in 1920.

A further report in the *Kentish Times* that Phil Babbs provided me with has no date, but it might have been the article I read back in the late 1960s that first got me interested in the Orpington car. It ran with the headline 'Car firm with loads of class' and was taken from a longer article that had already been published in a periodical entitled *Industry and Enterprise, Bromley Borough Local History No. 9.*

Unfortunately, I wasn't able to pinpoint a copy of either the publication or the article before this book went to print, but the abridged version in the local paper didn't cover anything new that hadn't already been published before or after that date. Except, that is, that this article finally recognised the fact that more than a dozen Orpingtons were made by confirming thus: 'Only 20 of the Orpington cars were produced between 1920 and 1925...'

'Only 20' is again a debatable point, but at least this figure is heading in the right direction. I go into this in a little more detail in the chapter headed *'How Many Orpingtons Were Really Made?'* which starts on page 89.

REPLIES TO THE *KENTISH TIMES* ARTICLE THAT WAS PUBLISHED ON 9 JANUARY 1959

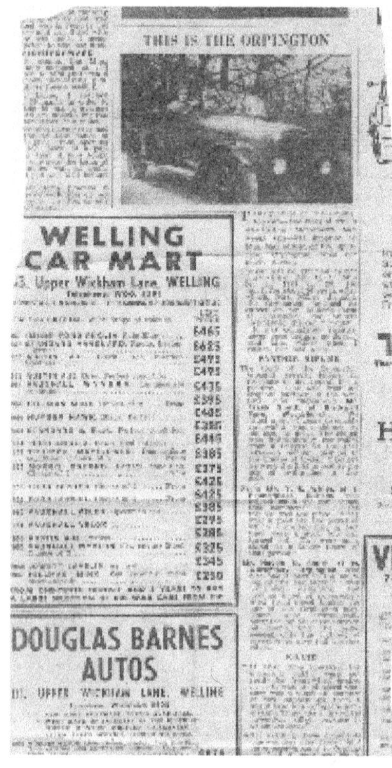

Following the article that was published in the *Orpington & Kentish Times*, in which the writer of the piece mentioned he couldn't find a picture of an Orpington (page 52), the newspaper published a photo of the car (*article image, left*) which was sent in by a Mrs May Miller. It was from her own private collection and, she explained, her husband had purchased the Orpington (nicknamed 'Trojan') in 1922 or 1923, he ran it for about ten years and then it was thought that it finished its life on Mr Miller's farm at

Chelsfield. "It was completely reliable, never once letting us down," Mrs Miller reportedly told the columnist who had visited her.

The very next comment printed on the page was from Frank Smith himself, which said, "We fitted a set of gears to enable an invalid – who could not use his legs – to drive. The clutch was hydraulically controlled from a trigger on the gear lever – in similar fashion to the brakes of today. I believe we were the first to realise the use of hydraulics in this field." (**see Observations on page 59).*

A Mr T S White of Eltham, who apparently helped to build Orpingtons wrote: "...the trouble was the price. They were a good car, the power of which surprised me; in fact they were a good job well turned out. Two were on a Motor Show of that period."

Mr Haydn Smith, whom I had discovered early on in my research was a young local lad at the time that the Smith & Milroy workshop was producing Orpingtons and had taken an interest in them, wrote and mentioned: "I well remember designing and making a set of power-operated front-wheel brakes for one of the Orpington cars. These were hydraulically operated by an engine-driven oil pump, and the pedal needed only the lightest of pressure to give full braking effort."

He continued: "At that time, however, the motoring public were not ready for front-wheel brakes... it was prophesised that they would cause all manner of dire happenings, from a slight skid to a complete somersault. Thus was a first-class invention killed because it came too soon." (**see Observations on page 59*).

Unfortunately, neither Frank Smith nor Haydn Smith (no relation) are with us any more, so they cannot provide any further answers to their comments or the questions they now raise.

I am, however, sure that the reporter who covered the story on 14 August 1980 had cross-referenced their own article with the one printed on 9 January 1959 and *assumed* that Haydn Smith's invention was for the adapted car when, in essence, it was for a one-off Orpington to try Haydn's front-braking system idea. An easy yet no doubt unintentional mistake for the reporter to make.

Observations

*This comment would seem to throw even more confusion into the adapted car melting pot. What *is* of significance is that Frank Smith *didn't* mention that the gears were fitted to an Orpington, which seems to me to suggest that the columnist who edited the letters page *wanted* the readers to believe it was an alteration done to an Orpington. Had an Orpington been involved, I am certain that Frank would have taken the opportunity to say so in his letter.

**Haydn Smith had apparently told a friend of his later in life that he was a young lad when the Orpington car was being produced. Aside from what he wrote to the *Kentish Times*, there is actually no confirmation that he was directly or indirectly involved with the building of the cars. Nor, for that matter, that he was even employed by the Smith & Milroy company. He may well have designed a front-wheel braking system, which Smith & Milroy Ltd may have agreed to try out on one of the Orpingtons, but there is no evidence linking this to the story about the adapted car for a disabled person (but please see the chapter, titled *'The Adapted Car – And What Really Happened'*, on page 79).

*A sales ad showing the Orpington with the boot open to display
the positioning of the dickey seat.
Picture courtesy of Frank Smith's family archives.*

THE RISE AND FALL OF THE ORPINGTON

This was the aptly-named title of an article written by Edward Babbs for the *Links* magazine, the bulletin of the Newcomen Society for the History of Engineering & Technology, in 2003.

Of all the articles I have read relating to the Orpington itself (aside from the more technical articles written by *The Motor* and *The Light Car and Cyclecar* magazines) during the course of my research, this one is the nearest to being factually correct. But then, I couldn't have expected anything else, as Mr Babbs is the nephew of Frank Smith by

virtue of the fact that he is Katie Scott-Murray's son.

However, as you will read on a later page, the information about an adapted Orpington car in Edward's article may have also been incorrectly recorded. I think this is more because of the fact that Edward may have taken his information from the previous local newspaper reports that are archived in the Bromley Library, whereas I have uncovered a document loaned to me by Mrs Pamela Moate (Frank Smith's grand-daughter and Edward Babbs' cousin) that strongly suggests it may not have been an Orpington that was adapted.

This is not to say that I wish to devalue Edward's work – far from it. His input via his excellent article has thrown up a couple of previously unpublished facts that I was also asking questions about before I read his account.

For instance, in the report published in the *Orpington & Kentish Times* newspaper on 9 January 1959, Jack Milroy was quoted as saying that there were no steep hills in or around the Orpington area upon which to trial the Orpington car. This quote was printed amid accusations that the Ford-made back axle was prone to overheating when climbing hills and customers who bought the car were apparently not made aware of this until afterwards, when they presumably broke down whilst climbing a gradient.

My immediate response to reading that interviewed report was "What about Polhill? What about Wrotham Hill?" They are both steep hills within a short travelling distance of Orpington High Street.

To my pleasant surprise, when I picked up and read through Edward's article, I noticed that he had covered this very fact, although he'd mentioned Westerham Hill instead of Wrotham Hill. Either way, there were (and still are) at least two steep hills in the Orpington vicinity that the car could have been trialled on, and I believe that Frank Smith would have taken the time to hill trial the Orpington given his meticulous approach to this project in all other aspects.

So, the question that really must be asked is, did Jack Milroy actually say those words to the local newspaper reporter, or did the reporter forget to ask the question and subsequently fabricated the bit about the lack of hills?

Additionally, I'm a bit surprised that the apparent axle overheating problem wasn't mentioned in the *Light Car and Cyclecar* hill test report dated 6 November 1920, unless it was an intermittent rather than an inherent fault that only happened every now and then.

Edward Babbs has also managed to clear up a contentious point, either by design or by accident, and that is regarding the legal entity of the Smith and Milroy business. When cousins Frank Smith and Jack Milroy first started up by building and repairing bicycles and motorcycles, they did so as a partnership: Smith & Milroy. The partnership existed all the while they were at Wellington Road in St Mary Cray. But (and my own research clarifies this), once they'd built and moved to the garage at the lower end of the High Street, opposite the Priory pond, the business became a limited company: Smith & Milroy Ltd.

Yet, still the various local newspaper reports referred to the car makers as a 'partnership'. Although perhaps not a major issue, per se, it is another example of how unreliable and contradictory the other articles' contents were.

For good measure, Edward also questioned and virtually blew out of the water the notion published in the earlier articles that only 12 Orpingtons were made. This figure is absolute rubbish and, as you'll read in the chapter entitled *'How Many Orpington Cars Were Really Made?'* starting on page 89, I even throw into question and doubt that the official figure of 'only 21' was correct. In Edward's account, he mentions that Katie (his mother) recalled there were about two dozen models that were built and sold. I have no reason to doubt that figure for *complete* Orpingtons created, but what about the number of *chassis-only* models that Smith & Milroy Ltd produced? They were known to build and sell the chassis separately to, and independently of, the assembled cars.

Sadly, as Edward adds to his article, "It is not thought that a single example [of the Orpington] survives and all that is left are a few yellowing newspaper clippings and photographs…"

I can certainly confirm what Edward says about the car not surviving, as I placed small ads and letters in several regional newspapers over the past four years, asking for anyone to come forward and show me proof that an Orpington car still exists. I have not had one single response. However, I did uncover a story that an Orpington allegedly once featured on TV in an episode of the now-defunct 'Crossroads' soap opera in the 1970s, but this is unsubstantiated at the time I write this account.

With regard to the second part, yes, the newspaper clippings I've seen and photocopied are yellowed through time. But I've also seen and read magazine articles (either photocopies or the actual magazines) and viewed an original Orpington car badge (reproduced in black and white on page 100 and in colour on the outer back cover of this book). And now there's this book to keep as a memento of a car long-forgotten, yet whose former existence has been rediscovered.

MR FRANK SMITH

There can be no disputing the fact that Frank Smith was the brains of the Smith and Milroy outfit. After all, it was his forethought that led to the design of the Orpington car.

However, he was not a draughtsman, so the blueprint for his design for the Orpington car was prepared by a Mr Linley, who later designed the first pre-selector gearbox.

Frank Smith poses for a photo with his 5 surviving sisters out of an original 7, circa 1960. Katie Scott-Murray stands fourth from the left in the long coat. Photo courtesy of Pamela Moate.

Rediscovering... The ORPINGTON Car

Frank, together with his cousin Jack Milroy, forged a solid business partnership in the early 20th century, firstly building and repairing bicycles and motorcycles from a small workshop in Wellington Road, St Mary Cray.

The inside of Frank Smith's workshop at Church Hill. Is that the front wheel and mudguard of an Orpington just visible through the far doorway...? Photo courtesy of Pamela Moate.

As the business gathered momentum, Frank and Jack purchased and built a much larger workshop at the bottom end of Orpington High Street, in 1912. In 1914, Frank also built a smaller garage in Church Hill, which was to be later used as an overspill building for the main business.

The Church Hill premises also had living accommodation incorporated on the first floor and this is where Frank, his wife Alice and their four children lived.

In the 1930s, the Smith & Milroy company was dissolved and Frank went to work at the Church Hill Garage until he and Alice bought Brickwall Farm at Woodchurch, Near Ashford, Kent in the early 1950s.

Church Hill Garage, Orpington, circa 1935. Alice Smith can just be made out looking from the upstairs window (above the fuel pumps). Photo courtesy of Pamela Moate.

Frank kept himself busy in retirement, running the farm and looking after his family, including his granddaughter Pamela who had also gone to live on the farm with her parents and grandparents.

Frank Smith was 82 when he died in 1963. We already know that at least one sister – Katie – survived him because she was interviewed by the *Orpington Times* reporter in 1980 when the revelation about the adapted car came to light. He was also survived by his wife Alice, three daughters and a son (Pamela Moate's father), granddaughter (Pamela Moate herself) and great-grandson.

Rediscovering... The ORPINGTON Car

A young Frank and Alice Smith with their three daughters. Their son hadn't been born at the time this photo was taken

An older Frank and Alice enjoying time out at Bexhill-on-Sea with their son and a daughter, circa 1950s. Photos courtesy of Pamela Moate

MISS KATIE SMITH

Katie Smith was Frank Smith's youngest sister. She was also one of the first women drivers in the UK.

In the early days of the Smith & Milroy business, Katie was employed there as an office clerk.

With the arrival of the First World War, which saw about half the Smith & Milroy workforce go off into battle, those staff members that had to remain were redeployed to the task of producing munitions and gun parts for the War effort.

Katie suddenly found that, by virtue of her motoring prowess, she was utilised to drive a van loaded with arsenal equipment from the Smith & Milroy factory in Orpington once a week to the War Office in London, a job she volunteered for, rather than got press-ganged into doing.

Rediscovering... The ORPINGTON Car

Katie with her first husband, Walter Babbs. The baby being held by Mr Babbs is their son, Edward Babbs. Photo courtesy of Phil Babbs.

Could this large panel van (showing Frank Smith's family holidaying in Osmington, Dorset, in the 1920s) have been used by Katie when she drove the munitions to London during the 1914-18 conflict?
Photo courtesy of Pamela Moate.

Katie survived two marriages. Her first was to local builder Walter Babbs on 1 June 1918, father of Edward Babbs. He died in 1938 aged 48. On 14 April 1940, Katie married Alfred Scott-Murray, a high-ranking Chief Engineer with North Kent Water Board. Alfred died in 1967, aged 84. Katie herself died in 1991 after reaching the grand age of 98.

When I was told of Katie's story, I was pretty much spellbound. Katie was a real-life heroine, somebody who had lived through and had experienced some amazing times, especially the First World War. It is a pity for me that I chose to research the Orpington car after Katie had died, because I am sure she would have been able to provide me with an exhilarating insight into what it was like to be entrusted with so much valuable cargo on her weekly trips to the centre of London.

Indeed, both Katie and her brother Frank would be two people at the top of my 'must meet' list, if ever that was possible.

MR JOHN 'JACK' MILROY

Through my research, I know that Jack was born and brought up in Stranraer on the Scottish west coast in the 1880s and 1890s. He moved south from the family home when he was in his early twenties, eventually linking up with his cousin Frank Smith in St Mary Cray.

I have learned from Phil Babbs, great nephew of Frank Smith, that Jack Milroy had a very laid back sort of personality and he would never let anything bother or worry him. Happy-go-lucky, in fact.

By contrast, Frank did all the worrying for the pair of them and the business, thus providing the level-headedness required to ensure a successful business. Both men encouraged harmony within the workplace.

Jack took membership of a number of 'light car' clubs in order to advertise the Orpington via several cross country and town trials and he won two medals for his achievements, a gold medal for the London to Edinburgh run and a silver medal for the London to Lands End run.

I have read an article, in an old motoring magazine from the 1990s, that stated Jack and Frank called time on their working partnership and Frank went and opened another garage (Church Hill Garage) further along Orpington High Street, allegedly 'in opposition to Milroy'. Sorry to have to disillusion the originator of (and anyone else who believes) that rumour but, that account is totally inaccurate and is based on pure conjecture; the two men remained the best of friends and were not in competition with each other.

The Smith & Milroy company *was* disbanded in the 1930s, and Frank *did* go and work at the Churchill Garage that he'd built in 1914, but it was *not* in competition with the larger business opposite the Priory pond. Both Frank and Alice lived in the apartment above the garage until they bought, and moved to, a farm in Kent.

Jack was one of a number of people to own an Orpington and he used it 'free of trouble and defects' for 15 years. The car was reported in one article as apparently having been broken up in 1930, although this could have been a misprint as 15 years on from 1920 was surely 1935, unless I've got my sums wrong!

During World War Two, Jack served in the Home Guard. He remained in the Orpington area and married late on in life. Both Jack and his wife lived in a bungalow in Oxendenwood Road, Chelsfield. They had no children, which is believed to be why his business at the Pond Garage finally closed down.

The Milroys' bungalow in Oxendenwood Road, Chelsfield, circa 2003.
Photo courtesy of Phil Babbs.

THE ADAPTED CAR – AND WHAT *REALLY* HAPPENED

In the *Orpington Times* article dated 14 August 1980, it mentioned as 'fact' something the reporter claimed, relating to Smith & Milroy Ltd adapting one of their Orpington cars for 'the handicapped [disabled] son of a rich Arab'. This inclusion now appears to be somewhat controversial, as I will now explain.

Please be assured that it is *not* my intention to point an accusing finger at anybody here, but I do have a moral obligation as a writer to firstly present all the known facts and, secondly, to try and make sure that the information I supply is correct.

To add credence to the fact that the newspaper article may be incorrect in materials particular, it also inaccurately stated that there were

> grey and using many standard Ford components—were made before conveyor-belt competition forced the Orpington off the roads.
>
> One was specially adapted for the handicapped son of a rich Arab—possibly the first use of hydraulics in clutch or brake systems. The last was produced around 1925.

only a dozen (12) vehicles [Orpingtons] made before 'conveyor belt competition forced the Orpington off the roads', which is a contentious issue.

The article from the 1980 issue of the *Orpington Times* is the first occasion that the news of an adapted Orpington car for 'the handicapped son of a rich Arab' has ever been so blatantly mentioned, although an indeterminately-worded letter from Frank Smith to the *Kentish Times* in 1959 makes reference to "we fitted a set of gears... " *(please see page 57)* without confirming it was an Orpington.

However, nestled amongst all the documentation that I went through, there was a typewritten note by one of Frank Smith's grown-up children which not only refutes what the reporter stated as fact, but goes into precise detail about what was really witnessed at the time.

I have reproduced that typewritten note here and, in case you have difficulty in reading the contents of the typing in the image, I have typed it all out again immediately underneath it. I have left the grammar and spelling exactly the same throughout.

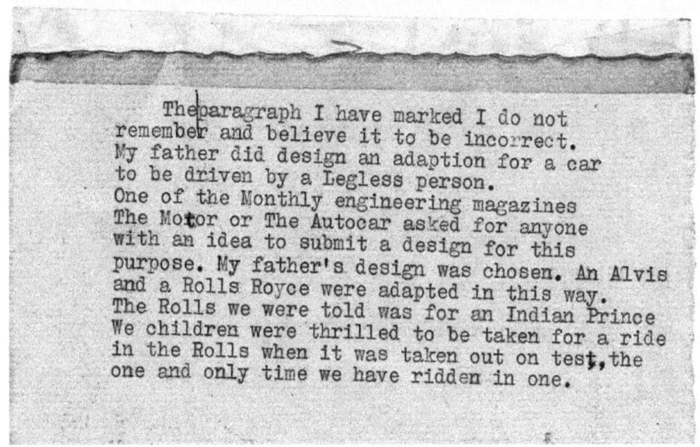

"The paragraph I have marked I do not remember and believe it to be incorrect. My father did design an adaption for a car to be driven by a Legless person.

One of the monthly engineering magazines The Motor or The Autocar asked for anyone with an idea to submit a design for this purpose. My father's design was chosen. An Alvis and a Rolls Royce were adapted in this way.

The Rolls we were told was for an Indian Prince We children were thrilled to be taken for a ride in the Rolls when it was taken out on test, the one and only time we have ridden in one."

The other interesting fact is, of course, that the car (a Rolls Royce) was apparently adapted for a disabled 'Indian Prince' and not 'the handicapped son of a rich Arab'. What version sounds more interesting? I'll leave you to decide.

When I first read the report in the *Orpington Times*, I wrongly attributed the information about the converted car to Katie Scott-Murray, as the reporter had been adding quotes from her in the body text of the article. However, whilst I was typing out this page, I took a very much closer look at that article and there is absolutely no qualifying quote about the matter from Katie. The reporter had stated it as fact, *not* a quote, that an Orpington had indeed been adapted for 'the handicapped son of a rich Arab'.

Consequently, I pulled back from the brink of doing Katie Scott-Murray a huge injustice, which would have unintentionally blamed her for stating something as fact about the Orpington that is now of questionable standing. Having been told by people who knew her well – her grandson and neice – what kind of person she was, I totally realise that Katie would not have deliberately or unintentionally misled the writer of the *Orpington Times* article and, equally, she would not have given the wrong information.

So, where did the reporter get the information from? I believe it was possible that Katie may have mentioned something in passing, but the end result leaves us with the probability that the reporter either misheard what Katie might have said about the adaption news or, they mistranscribed any trigger notes or shorthand taken at the time of (or after) the interview which culminated in this apparent inaccuracy being included in the article, hence why the information was stated as a fact rather than as a quote. In other words, the reporter didn't correctly record what was said and couldn't risk attributing it to anybody having said it – in this case, Katie Scott-Murray – perhaps on pain of losing their job.

Also, the letter from Haydn Smith that was printed in the 1959 article follow-up, may have influenced and misguided the reporter of the 1980 article.

Whichever it was, it resulted in a false positive being recorded as fact and it was unwittingly copied as such into subsequent articles written about the Orpington. A sort of literary Chinese Whispers.

However, since that 'fact' has been printed, further articles on the Orpington have followed suit, undoubtedly without the writers first checking its accuracy. There's no disputing the fact that Smith & Milroy Ltd *did* adapt a car, but *not* an Orpington, and that it was for the disabled relative of a foreign dignitary.

In the typewritten manuscript, which was created in 1980 as a direct response to the article dated 14 August 1980, there are references to 'my father' which, it can be safely said, confirms that it was 'penned' (typed) by one of Frank Smith's (by then grown up) children.

It is known that Jack Milroy married late in life and he had no children, so the references to 'my father' wouldn't have been relating to him, which only leaves Frank Smith's family, hence why it was in his family's possession.

Unfortunately, the typewritten piece hasn't been signed or dated, but then I doubt very much it crossed the originator's mind at the time that the statement could eventually have a future importance on the history of the Orpington car. I also have no doubts about the authenticity of the typed document, because when I first saw it it was stuck on to a clipping of the newspaper article by very worn out and faded sticky tape. So it wasn't a recent addition.

Nevertheless, it is a statement that cannot be dismissed out of hand, and this is why I felt that it was an item too valuable to leave out of this book.

Another significance of the typewritten account is the mention of experiencing a once-in-a-lifetime ride in a Rolls Royce, on a test run, after it had been adapted. When I first uncovered and read that statement, I was hit by the excitement that the writer portrayed, as a child would have experienced, of riding in a Rolls Royce, and it has left me in little doubt that they had travelled as described and then consequently recalled the incident with clarity and accuracy many years later.

In comparison, I have yet to travel in a Rolls Royce myself. But, if or when I ever do, I'd like to believe that the memory will stay with me for the rest of my life. Just like it obviously did for Frank Smith's offspring.

So, what *is* the real story of the adapted car? Well, Frank Smith *did* design - and Smith & Milroy Ltd *did* adapt - *a car* for a disabled person from overseas. But, whilst it is impressive to assume it may have been an

Orpington car that had been adapted, in reality a 'rich Arab' or a 'legless Indian Prince' would have opted for an internationally-renowned marque in preference to a little-known locally manufactured alternative.

After all, money would have been no object, be it for a 'rich Arab' or an 'Indian Prince'. Otherwise, would they have been able to afford an adaption to a car in the first place? In a word, *no*.

The mention of Haydn Smith's hydraulic front-wheel braking system is a red herring, in relation to the adapted car for the overseas customer, but the mention of it in his letter to the *Kentish Times* in 1959 maybe had an ambitious and zealous local reporter barking up the wrong tree in 1980, probably with good intent, and caused them to wrongly attribute the adaption to an Orpington instead of a Rolls Royce.

Indeed, the reporter of the 1980 version of events would have had access to the article and follow-up letters of 1959, probably leading to the misunderstanding about what car was actually adapted.

So, there we have it. Much how the *reported* version of the adaption story would have us believe that one of the Orpingtons had been adapted, the truth is rather less romantic.

HOW MANY ORPINGTONS WERE *REALLY* MADE?

Throughout my extensive studying of the existing documentation relating to this car, I kept coming up against a similar story, which stated that Smith and Milroy only built around 21 to 24 Orpingtons. But I believe that it depends on what is considered the 'build' aspect. If, as I suspect is the case, the writers of previous articles of the car have only taken into account the amount of cars with an Orpington body then, yes, maybe the company did only produce 21 to 24 cars in total between 1920 and 1924.

Bearing in mind what has been said and written in earlier chapters of this book about the *chassis* being offered and sold separately, we have to look at the matter of how many Orpingtons were *really* built in a new light. If, as I have already mentioned, the Smith and Milroy workshop built the same chassis, as used for the Orpington, for other bodywork designers to use then the limit of 21 to 24 vehicles placed upon Orpington production may be wildly short of the actual figure. After all, the Smith and Milroy business was run successfully for many, many years and they employed a large staff base, so it would be remiss of anyone to think that they only repaired vehicles after the demise of the Orpington-bodied car. What we also have to consider is the fact that, without a chassis, a car's body could not function (notwithstanding later designs).

Car chassis would have still been required after 1924. The Smith and Milroy workshop was fitted with all the tools and apparatus needed to continue producing chassis designed by Frank Smith. The staff were fully trained up to produce precision-engineered chassis. What would have been simpler than Smith & Milroy Ltd continuing in this vein and avoiding the need for redundancies?

The Orpington was first displayed at the 1920 Motor Show in London (Stand 311 at the White City). Any number of other garages or bodywork designers could have placed orders for the Orpington's chassis, leading to accounts for the assembly of many hundreds – maybe thousands – to be produced.

Due consideration must be given to the fact that, it is not beyond the realms of probability for the Orpington to have continued to be manufactured beyond 1924, in the guise of its chassis.

Unless the accounts records and work orders for Smith and Milroy can be produced from the production years of the Orpington car then we will never know the true extent of how many Orpington chassis were *really* built.

So, what did cause the downfall of the Orpington?

Part of the eventual downfall of the Orpington was probably due to the later price that I found, as it made the Orpington much more expensive than cars of a similar ilk being produced by companies that were later to become household names around the world.

An example of this, which I found a reference to, was a 1924 Morris being £54 (to coin a phrase, 'a lot of money in those days') less expensive than an Orpington.

PREVIOUSLY UNPUBLISHED PHOTOS OF ORPINGTONS

Interesting things get unearthed when research is undertaken, and my work on the Orpington car history is no exception. By pure accident, I have uncovered some previously-unpublished photos of Orpingtons. I have reproduced them in this chapter.

Picture courtesy of Frank Smith's family archives.

The first picture (above) is of an Orpington travelling along Farnborough Hill, near

Orpington. This captures a more balmy time in rural England during the early part of the 20th century, a time that has sadly drifted away into the past.

Alongside the Orpington can be seen a steam traction engine and a horse-drawn cart. The row of shops in the background, all with their shutter blinds fully extended, indicate that it was a sunny day, as blinds such as these were often used to protect produce in the shop windows from the sun's rays.

The car in this next photo (below) is also believed to be an Orpington, this time viewed from the rear.

The rounded shape of the boot hid the 'secret'

of the dickey seat on the four-seater version of the car. On the two-seater model, it would have been all boot space.

The next photograph (below) was taken as an Orpington was travelling along Station Approach in the town, and looks very much like the picture was turned into a postcard, judging from the inscription in the bottom left corner.

This picture was kindly forwarded to me by Phil Waller, who runs the Orpington History website, for inclusion in this book. This is another one of those unique finds and I am pretty sure that this photo has never been published before in relation to an article on the Orpington car.

It's a bit of a nuisance that I don't know who the drivers were in these photos; they could be the car owners or, possibly, they could be Smith & Milroy Ltd staff members out and about getting publicity shots for the car itself.

IS IT OR ISN'T IT?

<u>Not</u> an Orpington. Photo courtesy of www.prewarcar.com

Ah, now I've thrown this next one in *(above)* because it is *not* an Orpington! There was much debate on a website page at www.prewarcar.com when I was researching this subject, and two visitors to the site were adamant that the car in the photo was an Orpington. At the time of writing, alas, I also noticed that at least one more website is displaying the very same photo and still claiming it to be an Orpington.

There are several indicators that are shouting out at me from the photo, most notably the length and shape of the car and the 'generous' ground clearance of the bodywork. The era is right, 1920s, but the car is most definitely *not* an Orpington.

Firstly, the wheelbase is too long. A proper Orpington was shorter in length and was compact. Secondly, the car in the picture on page 97 has two rows of seats in the main body of the car. The four seater Orpington had the second set of seats in the boot (the dickey). Thirdly, the wheels are not right for an Orpington. Frank Smith and Jack Milroy always used spoke-visible wheels without trims or hubcaps.

In association with Phil Babbs, I have also managed to get confirmation from Edward Babbs that it is very definitely <u>not</u> an Orpington and, in addition to this, none of the documentation provided to me by Pamela Moate has made any reference to, or about, the car in the picture on page 97. In other words, the labelling of it as an Orpington is purely incorrect guesswork on the part of ill-informed motor car 'experts'. Have I 'won' the discussion...?

Radiator grilles were much of a muchness back in the 1920s, most tending to follow the example set by the Ford Motor Company. The grille shown in the photo on page 97 is very similar to that of the Orpington but, as can be seen here, it also resembles the Model T Ford grille (below). In fact, this Model T looks remarkably similar to the 'pretend' Orpington on page 97 that I'd almost go as far as to say that they are one and the same model, one with the soft-top roof down and the other with it up.

THE SOLE SURVIVING ORPINGTON CAR BADGE

This is the only known surviving part of an Orpington car.

Finished in royal blue and gold enamel on an oval brass base, this now unique relic is housed at the Bromley Museum.

A smaller, full colour version of this badge image can be seen on the outside back cover of this book.

Orpington bonnet badge image reproduced with kind permission of the Bromley Meseum Service. Photo: Copyright ©2012 Bromley Museum Service.

SO, WHERE *IS* ORPINGTON?

Orpington is a densely populated town that is in *postal* Kent but, because of the way the Greater London boundary now engulfs more outlying peripheral areas of the Capital, it is now part of 'South London'.

Situated about 15 miles south-east of the centre of London, Orpington is central to the triangle of towns of Bromley, Dartford and Sidcup.

The town of Orpington is probably most famously known for the 1962 by-election when the

Liberal Party (Eric Lubbock, MP) gained the seat in a surprise victory over the Conservatives. In addition to this, Orpington boasts association with such famous people as Gary Rhodes *(TV Chef)* and the late Jeremy Beadle *(Television Presenter)*. Charles Darwin

(author of 'Origin of Species') lived most of his life at Downe, just outside of Orpington.

The most recognised football club from the area is Cray Wanderers FC, which was founded in nearby St Mary Cray in 1860, making it the second-oldest association football club in the world, the oldest in Kent and nowadays (due to the shifting tides of the Greater London boundary) also the oldest in London.

Orpington is also renowned for its own breed of chicken which was created by William Cook in 1886. The original version was black in colour but, over  the century and a quarter since then, the black Orpington has given way to the bird with buff coloured feathers. There is also another strain which has white feathers. The white Orpington was introduced about three years after the original black feathered variety. For those readers who are truly interested, the black Orpington was a crossbreed between Minorcas, Plymouth Rock and Langshan hens, whilst the white was a cross between a White Leghorn, Black Hamburg and a White Dorking. Queen Elizabeth The Queen Mother was known to have kept examples of the Buff Orpington.

More information on the history of Orpington can be found on the dedicated website at **www.Orpington-History.org**.

EPILOGUE

Well, you've now read everything that I have learnt and know about the Orpington car.

I have covered many miles, be they physically, through the internet or on the telephone, with the main purpose of finally bringing the true facts to light and laying the assumptions and guesswork of other articles to rest.

No doubt there will still be some self-styled 'experts' among us who think they know different to what has taken me nearly four years of painstaking study to properly find out; people who won't particularly like the real story behind the Orpington car.

My resources, based on fact, have reliably come from the actual families of the people directly behind this iconic vehicle, and the precious documentation and photographs that they have kept down the years, *not* from hearsay or 'expert advice' from anyone who was not actually associated or involved with Smith & Milroy Ltd in the 1920s.

I have tried to be as thorough as I possibly can with acknowledging the people and organisations that have helped me in my quest, and I am especially grateful to the living direct descendants of Frank Smith – in particular Phil Babbs, Pamela Moate and Edward Babbs.

This is a story and recollection of a bygone age that needed so much to be updated and corrected and I am pleased to have had the chance to do just that.

I hope that you have enjoyed reading this account and that you will keep it on your bookshelf for future reference.

The Orpington – a legend in its own lifetime.

ABOUT THE AUTHOR

Trevor Mulligan was born in Farnborough Hospital, situated between Orpington and Bromley, in the 1950s. He spent all of his younger and teen years growing up in St Mary Cray and Orpington.

A student of St Mary Cray Primary School, Poverest Junior School and Walsingham Secondary Boys' School in the 1960s, Trevor abandoned his education to join the Civil Service in early 1971, aged just 15 years.

In 1981, Trevor moved away from the area, but still maintains links through his association with Cray Wanderers Football Club, and some of his family members still live thereabouts.

After 38 turbulent years in his job, Trevor was granted early retirement in 2009 and is now a full-time Carer for his wife Myra, who contracted a progressive disabling illness in 1999. They live near the seaside at Folkestone in Kent.